# Sunshine's Excellent Adventures

Reggie and Anita Hill

ISBN 978-1-64028-213-1 (Paperback)
ISBN 978-1-64028-214-8 (Digital)

Christian Faith Publishing, Inc.
296 Chestnut Street
Meadville, PA 16335
www.christianfaithpublishing.com

Printed in the United States of America

# Sunshine's First Home

Sunshine's first home was underneath a big pier. It was an exciting place that was home to many interesting characters that soon became Sunshine's friends. Among them were Claude Crab, Polly Pelican, and Sam Seagull.

Each of Sunshine's friends were special. Claude Crab would sometimes run sideways when he got excited. Polly Pelican had a huge mouth and smiled a lot when it was full of fish. Sam Seagull could perch on top of a small post without falling down!

Sunshine's mom was called Momma Motley. She was very proud of Sunshine and how easily he could make friends. One day, she asked Sunshine his secret for making friends so easily. Sunshine told Momma Motley that the best way to make friends was to treat them exactly the way that he wanted to be treated. He said friends listen to one another, play together, and try to make each other happy whenever either is sad.

Sunshine's first home was his first excellent adventure.

# Sunshine's New Home

Now Sunshine had many brothers and sisters. Momma Motley worried about all her kittens having enough food to eat. She wanted her babies to be well fed, happy, and healthy.

One day the pier owner, Mr. Kip, found Sunshine wandering around on the pier. He saw that Sunshine was skinny and needed more food. Mr. Kip remembered that there were two people named Anita and Reggie who wanted to adopt a kitten to care for and love. Mr. Kip knew that Anita and Reggie would be very interested in Sunshine because he was special. Sunshine was special because he had an extra toe on each paw! His little feet looked like a baseball catcher's mitt!

Mr. Kip picked up Sunshine, placed him in a big box, and then called Anita and Reggie. Anita and Reggie came down to the pier, got Sunshine, and took him to their beach house. From that day on, Sunshine had plenty of food, love, and a new big clean home. Sunshine could even hear the ocean from his new home, which reminded him of Momma Motley and all his pier friends.

Momma Motley was happy for her Sunshine and his good luck. She hoped that her other kittens would find good homes also.

Sunshine's new home was his next excellent adventure.

# Sunshine's Friend Jack

Across the street from Summerhill, Sunshine's beach house, is the home of Jack the artist. Now Jack is a wonderful man who can paint beautiful pictures of anything!

One day, Jack walked over to visit Anita and Reggie. On that special day, Jack met Sunshine for the first time. He held Sunshine and told him that he was a beautiful kitty and special because of his little mitten paws. Jack asked Anita and Reggie if he could borrow a photo of Sunshine so they gave him one to take home with him.

Several weeks later, Jack came over for another visit. In his hands was a gift for Sunshine, Reggie, and Anita. It was a beautiful portrait of Sunshine that Jack had painted. The portrait looked exactly like Sunshine and now hangs on the wall in a special place at Lakewood, Sunshine's country home.

Making friends with Jack the artist was Sunshine's next excellent adventure.

# Sunshine's First Excellent Trick

One day, Sunshine was playing with a piece of candy wrapped in crinkly paper. Sunshine loved the sound the paper made when he batted the candy around the room.

Anita and Reggie were laughing as they watched Sunshine play with his candy. All of the sudden, Sunshine decided to pick up the candy with his mouth, run to Anita, and place it on her toes. When he did this, Anita squealed with delight. Sunshine realized that this was an excellent game to play since it was fun for both him and Anita.

The next thing that happened was even more amazing. Anita picked up the candy off her toes, tossed it across the room, and said, "Fetch!" to Sunshine. Little Sunshine then dashed across the room, picked up the candy with his mouth again, ran across the room, and placed it on Anita's toes. Anita squealed with delight, picked up Sunshine, hugged him, and told him he was a "good boy." Sunshine loved to hear "good boy," so he decided to "fetch" from now on whenever Anita asked him too.

Sunshine's first trick was his next excellent adventure.

# Sunshine's Doctor Friend

All of us get sick from time to time—even Sunshine. When Sunshine doesn't feel good, it's time for a visit with his friend Doctor Barker.

Doctor Barker is a very kind veterinarian who loves all animals. He has several helpers in his office who are also kind and love to care for sick little animals of all types. One of these helpers is named Sheri, and she especially loves Sunshine and Sunshine loves her.

Sunshine knows that Doctor Barker and his helpers are eager to make Sunshine feel better when he is sick. So Sunshine doesn't mind going to visit them even though it can be a little scary since it is not his home. Sunshine says that we should all appreciate our doctor friends and not be afraid to see them when we don't feel well.

Sunshine says that visiting the doctor is just another excellent adventure.

# Sunshine's First Christmas

Sunshine, Anita, and Reggie left Summerhill, the beach house and returned to Lakewood, the country home, to celebrate Christmas.

This was Sunshine's very first Christmas. All of Reggie's family came to Lakewood on Christmas day for dinner and presents. Everyone of Reggie's family saw Sunshine for the first time and immediately loved him. Janice, Reggie's sister, who always loved and had kittens, especially loved Sunshine. She loved him so much that a few months later, Reggie brought Janice one of Sunshine's brothers from a later litter that Momma Motley had under the pier. The new kitten was solid white and so beautiful. Janice named him Bubba. Momma Motley was again happy that one of her kittens had a safe new home.

Sunshine had a wonderful time playing with all the crinkly paper-wrapped presents under the Christmas tree. Every time someone opened a present, they would toss the paper on the floor, and Sunshine would jump on it and play! Everyone received wonderful presents, including Sunshine.

This was Sunshine's next excellent adventure.

# Sunshine's Beach Home

Sunshine, Anita, and Reggie have a wonderful little beach house called Summerhill. It is on the beautiful North Carolina coast and one of Sunshine's favorite places.

Summerhill is a little cottage with flowers, trees, and fences that Sunshine describes as "purrfect." it is near the ocean so Sunshine thinks about his first pier home and Momma Motley whenever he stays at Summerhill. He can smell the salt air and yummy fish and that makes him so happy.

There are several other kitties that live in the Summerhill neighborhood. One is a big, black and white kitty whose name is Tom. Sometimes he will walk up to Sunshine's front door, look in, and say hello to Sunshine. Whenever he does, Sunshine thinks about how wonderful it is to have friends.

Sunshine says that good friends are like an excellent adventure!

# Sunshine's Daily Chore

Like everyone big and small, Sunshine had a daily chore to do. Sunshine's chore was to do something every day to make Anita and Reggie laugh!

Sunshine could always be counted on to retrieve every time a crinkly paper-covered candy was tossed across the room. Time and again, he would fetch the candy and place it on either Anita's or Reggie's foot, depending on who tossed it.

Sometimes Sunshine would surprise Anita and Reggie with a new trick. One day, Anita went shopping and Reggie and Sunshine stayed home. They came up with a new surprise trick that day. When Anita returned home, Reggie and Sunshine were waiting for her in the kitchen. When she walked into the kitchen, Reggie said, "Cute boy" to Sunshine, and lo and behold, Sunshine immediately lay down on his side near Anita's feet, curled his big mitten paws and looked up at her. Anita squealed with delight and said that this was the best trick ever!

Sunshine's "cute boy" trick was his next excellent adventure.

# Sunshine's Friend Speedy the Squirrel

One day at Lakewood, Sunshine's country home, he was sitting by the window looking out across the deck at the lake. All of a sudden, a gray squirrel ran past the window. He was running so fast that Sunshine could barely see him.

A few minutes later, the squirrel ran over and stopped right in front of Sunshine! They looked at each other and smiled. He was so fast that Sunshine decided to name him Speedy.

Sometime later, Reggie came home with exciting news. He told Anita and Sunshine that he had seen this wonderful gray squirrel near Lakewood's apple orchard. The squirrel had jumped out of an apple tree with an apple in his mouth and ran past Reggie. This was the fastest squirrel that Reggie had ever seen!

Sunshine secretly knew that the squirrel Reggie saw was speedy! Sunshine was happy that Reggie had seen his wonderful friend Speedy. He hoped that Speedy enjoyed eating the apple and picked many more from the orchard.

This was Sunshine's next excellent adventure.

# About the Authors

Reggie and Anita attended school together from first grade through graduation. They were married forty-seven years ago while Reggie served in the US Army Security Agency. They spent their first two years of marriage in Japan and loved the culture and Japanese people.

Both Reggie and Anita love all animals, especially cats. Sunshine added so much joy and fun to both their lives as a companion and playmate. Career-wise, Anita has been a teacher, banker, and real estate professional. Reggie has had successful careers as a technology consultant, professor, and financial advisor.

Anita's hobbies are growing orchids and bird watching. Reggie enjoys fishing, writing poetry, and as of late, learning how to play the mandolin and banjo. They enjoy dividing their time between their farm Lakewood in the North Carolina Piedmont and Cranberry, their stone cottage in the North Carolina Mountains. Both Reggie and Anita love to travel and have taken many wonderful and memorable trips over the years. Reggie and Anita were never able to have children, and it is their sincere wish that *Sunshine's Excellent Adventures* will bring joy to children everywhere.